The Enigma of Imagination

Exploring the Intriguing Paths of Creativity

"You cannot exhaust your creativity. The more you use, the more you have."

Maya Angelou

"Creativity is intelligence

having fun."

Albert Einstein

"The creative mind plays with

the objects it loves."

Carl Jung

"We're so creative that when we don't have problems, we make them up."

Augusto Cury

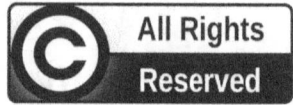

For a long time I had the belief that creativity was associated with a great idea, an invention. But over the years, I discovered that creativity comes from combining a set of elements - experiences, information, references... - to solve problems or even fulfill desires.

No good idea comes by chance.

It always comes after another one that arose before the moment when it could be realized.

Everyone is creative!

Everyone is born with the possibility to create, to find solutions. But we unlearn it. We fall into molds - the first is school. You need to respond according to templates, with standards.

Creativity is an attempt to deconstruct a set of beliefs that you are not creative, that you will follow an assembly line, you will fit into a box. You need to unlearn patterns, form new beliefs, to relearn to create.

Creativity is and will increasingly be the main differentiating factor of human beings.

Enjoy reading!

summary

- Training the brain to be more creative

- how to connect ideas

- 7 blocks to creative thinking and how to solve them

- Mental Drainage

- Campo Mental

- Roadmap to boost creativity

- the google case

- Creativity Methods

- compass technique

- Brainstorm

- challenging assumptions

- opposite technique

- The human being is not the traveler, he is the path

Training the brain to be more creative

Abandon routines.

Your brain needs fuel and needs to be stretched to create those "OMG!" moments on demand.

Think about it. Great athletes train their bodies for days, weeks and years to push them to peak performance. Why, then, wouldn't a breeder do the same with his brain?

I've spent a decade (and counting) in the advertising industry, and contrary to popular belief, creativity is not inherent. You have to improve it. Over time, I figured out what I need to do to get ideas flowing freely, and a lot of that insight comes from my interest in neuroscience. The more we learn about how our gray matter works, the better we can train it, control it, and make it do what we want.

Here are some things that have worked for me over the years.

Contact with nature. And withproved that spending time in nature makes us more creative. Looking at trees and leaves – instead of our electronic devices – reduces our anxiety, slows our heart rate, calms us down and allows our brain to make connections more easily.

By spending time in nature, I am also not referring to a hike in the desert. Walking in an urban green space for just 25 minutes can calm our brains and help us shift into the node of autopilot. According to the British Journal of Sports Medicine, this state awakens our current consciousness and fuels the imagination. We are more easily able to connect existing notions, thoughts and images to form a new, relevant and usable concept.

So make disconnection a priority. Take a walk in your neighborhood park, stroll along the beach, or just add plants to your porch and spend some time outside. For me, walking my dog. You'll feel the benefits of moving away from screens almost immediately.

Meditate. I know, I know, you've heard it a million times: Meditation clears our minds of muddled thoughts and gives our brain space to observe and reflect, improving focus on tasks and enhancing our ability to make smart decisions.

But did you know that meditation also puts the whole brain to work?

You may have heard that creativity uses the right side of the brain while the left brain is engaged during more analytical tasks. Well, neuroscientists have discovered that creativity actually resides in your entire brain – and meditation can give you access to it.

This intentional practice can be as simple as closing your eyes and focusing on your breath. Headspace, the popular meditation app, even has guided meditations to inspire creativity. The idea is that when we intentionally stop in awareness, we allow our minds the freedom and space to be quiet and creative. I practice this between meetings. I find a quiet space, focus on my breathing, and get my brain into an alpha, or waking state of relaxation. This allows me to disconnect from my initial ideas (after all, the human brain is programmed to follow the path of least resistance) and create new paths in my mind.

Move yourself. Steve Jobs was a big advocate of walking meetings for a reason. Movement has been linked to increased performance on creative tests. Exercise releases endorphins – chemicals our bodies produce to relieve stress and pain. When we are less stressed, our brains venture into more fruitful territories.

In fact, a recent article compared the chemical our brain releases during physical activity to Miracle-Gro, the water-soluble plant food that helps plants grow bigger and healthier. The good part is that getting around is super simple to do, especially when you're working from home. I often attend meetings while pedaling a stationary bike or planning short walks in between (and this can also be done in an office).

Try to add workout time into your calendar and make sure you don't skip it. If you feel like you don't have time for a dedicated workout, block 20 minutes in your schedule and spend that time doing stretches at your desk.

Connect with different types of people. When consciously seeking inspiration, enough cannot be said about diversity. Remember the brain and its predisposition to take the lazy route? Diversity makes the brain work harder by challenging stereotypes. Additionally, researchers at Johns Hopkins University have found that "exposure to diversity experiences can promote the development of more complex forms of thinking, including the ability to think critically."

I make a point of surrounding myself with people who come from backgrounds different from mine, because their perspectives are a catalyst for creative thinking. Contrasting opinions open up new possibilities and allow us to make connections we haven't seen before, leading to better decisions. There was something to be said for Abraham Lincoln filling his cabinet with a "team of rivals". Productive discussions, brainstorms and debates often result in wiser outcomes. At my agency, we've created an "inspiration board," which brings our people together from multiple regions, cultures, genders, and more, to initiate these kinds of discussions.

Today, the distributed work model born out of the pandemic has made it even easier to bring people together. I recommend using social media channels like LinkedIn and Instagram to follow and connect with people who have different backgrounds and experiences than your own. Don't limit yourself to geography when connecting with someone or expanding your network. We are much better at creative problem solving when we don't have the comfort of knowing what to expect, which can happen if we just surround ourselves with people like us.

Use these neuroscience principles to give your brain the exercise it needs. He will get you out of any rut. Or stop you from getting into one in the first place.

how to connect ideas

Everything you write is a story. A story you tell one, or many, people. It could be a statement, a report full of numbers, a lawsuit, or the fable of the 3 little pigs. So that your stories are well understood and not boring, keep in mind that the writing is a sequence of [...]

...

..

.

ideas glued together, by logic.

This is not a rule imposed by grammar; this is simply how we communicate; this is how we understand what we read.

For this, the language offers us many resources. Connectors are one of the most important because they link the parts of a text together. They are elements that make the story progress by giving clues for the reader to build meaning. He reads smoothly, until the end, without suffering, without brain gymnastics.

When thinking that a citizen can buy medicine in supermarkets, convenience stores and the like, I see that there is no reason to be favorable, even if they are only those that dispense a medical prescription. Of course it would be good, in times of hustle and bustle, for the family to be able to supply their home with all kinds of merchandise where everything is sold. Also, with more outlets, the price could drop. But I understand that this does not compensate for the risk to people's health and lives.

See how the hooks used connect one sentence to another creating different meanings:

When thinking – conveys the idea of time. Similar hooks: when, after, before, then, until, then, while.

Even though – accept/permit/grant. Other options: even though, even though, even though, even though.

Of course – agree/confirm. Synonyms: evidently, certainly, naturally, without a doubt.

Where - place. Synonyms: beside, on, to the left, in that place, in the middle, the place where, where it took place.

Also/E – add, group. More hooks: and, in addition, and yet, also, as well as, in the same way.

Did you see how connecting ideas well is important to give the text meaning?

The challenge is knowing how to choose the right connectors for each situation. But don't get hung up on them, let them flow.

7 blocks to creative thinking and how to solve them

Each of us has the power to be creative. It is part of our natural make-up as human beings. The problem is that we often block our natural creativity and thus make mistakes in thinking and give ourselves more problems than we should. Here are 7 ways to unlock your natural creativity and keep those channels unblocked.

1. Don't make assumptions.

Assumptions are examples of lazy thinking. We simply don't expect to get all the information we need to come to the right conclusions. There's the story of the bank customer who, after cashing a check and turning to leave, comes back and says, "Sorry, I think you made a mistake." The cashier responds, "Sorry, but there's nothing I can do. You should have told us. Once you're gone, we're not responsible anymore." To which the customer responds, "Well, that's fine. Thanks for the extra $40."

Tip: When you feel like jumping to conclusions, wait until you have all the information.

2. See things from other points of view.

A truly open mind is willing to accept that not only do other people have other points of view as valid as your own, but that those other points of view may be more valid. The story is told that the modernist painter Pablo Picasso was traveling by train through Spain when he spoke with a wealthy businessman who despised modern art. As proof that modern art does not adequately represent reality, he took a picture of his wife from his wallet and said, "This is what my wife should look like, not in some silly stylized representation". Picasso took the photo, studied it for a few moments, and asked, "Is this your wife?" The businessman nodded proudly. "She is very small," Picasso remarked wryly.

Tip: Don't have a monopoly on how things are. Things are not always what they seem. Be ready to consider other points of view.

3. Don't think like a yo-yo

Some people tend to have a tendency to go from a highly positive mood one minute to a highly negative one the next, all because of what they see in front of them. It's like a yo-yo: up one minute, down the next. It's much healthier to remain neutral and not let emotions get the better of you.

Tip: Remember that things are rarely as good - or as bad - as you think they are.

4. Get rid of thinking habitslazy.

Habit can be a major obstacle to clear thinking and another example of laziness. Try this experiment. Write down the Scottish surnames Macdonald, Macpherson and Macdougall and ask someone to pronounce them. Now follow with the word Machinery and see what happens. Most people probably pronounce it wrong. This is because we tend to think habitually and we don't like what doesn't fit.

Hint: Don't assume that just because things happened a certain way once, they will happen again.

5. Don't think like an old person, think like a child.

Research shows that the number of synapses, or connections, in the brain is greater in a two-year-old than in an average adult. The reason for this is that while a two-year-old doesn't have a limiting worldview, as adults we do. It is like a sculptor who starts with a large block of clay, more than he needs, and then gradually removes the clay as he shapes his sculpture. If we use our brain like a child, accepting everything without judgment, we can actually stop and reverse the brain aging process.

Tip: Don't worry about the age myth. With the right stimulation and a passion for learning, you can really boost your brain powers.

6. See the details, but also see "the big picture".

You may know John Godfrey Saxe's poem called "The blind men and the elephant". This tells how six blind men go to see an elephant and each one tries to find out what it is by touching it. One blind man touches the prey, another the trunk, another the tail, and so on. Of course, not being able to see the whole elephant, they come to completely different conclusions.

Tip: Try to keep the big picture in front of you while looking at the details. It will help put everything in its proper place and context.

7. Think for yourself.

Taking time to think is still frowned upon in many organizations that value activity over creativity. People who work in creatively constrained organizations tend to think the way they're supposed to think, or the way others think, or the way they've always thought. It's like the blind thought that*Hans Christian Anderson* describes in his story of "The Emperor's New Clothes". Everyone on earth refuses to see that the emperor is naked and has been led to believe that he is wearing splendid attire for his coronation. Only a young man who has been sick and has not participated in the cultural brainwashing can see the truth and shout: "Look, everyone, the Emperor has no clothes!"

Tip: Don't let others tell you how to think. When others ask for your opinion, tell them directly.

Once you make these 7 techniques part of your habitual thinking patterns, you'll be amazed at how easy it is to find new, innovative, and creative solutions to all of life's problems.

Mental Drainage

Get a notebook: every morning, you should write three pages with everything that comes to mind. Anything, for example: I have to take the car in for repairs. Come to think of it, there are some good things out there that I can do while
I fix the car.

There is no wrong way to write the pages, or right sequence. The pages do not have to be a literary work. Just that you understand them.

Nothing is too beautiful, silly, stupid or weird to include. Drop the idea of ridicule and let go of whatever comes to mind.
The morning pages are non-negotiable: don't skimp, don't skimp, don't care what your mood is or what your inner sensor says. Simply do it and check the results.

Campo mental

We are all part of one big energy field. One of the laws of energy is this: Energy of a certain kind or vibration tends to attract energies of the same type.

Thoughts and feelings have their own magnetic energy, which attracts energy of a similar nature.
This principle states that everything you do will eventually be reflected and come back to you.

We reap what we sow.

Close your eyes and relax deeply. Now recall any pleasant experiences you have had in the last few days.
Then imagine yourself in some country setting. Think about the details of the environment, creating them in your imagination the way you like *(it is very important that you do this, even if it seems silly at first sight)*.

Our fears arise from the things we are unwilling to face.

Set your goals. Create a well-defined idea or mental image. Focus on it regularly. Send him positive energy. Try to intensify the feeling that what you want really exists and is obtainable.

Recognize your own merits and congratulate yourself, without forgetting to express your gratitude for having fulfilled your desire.

Here are some important reminders regarding affirmative sentences:

Always use affirmative sentences in the present tense. It's important to act as if what you want is already a reality.

As a rule of thumb, the shorter and simpler an affirmation is, the more effective it will be. Don't forget that by doing the affirmations you are creating something new.

The purpose of affirmations is not to deny or try to change your feelings or emotions.

When using affirmations, do your best to believe what you are saying.

In this way, we recover all our spiritual strength, our inner emptiness is filled from within and we transform ourselves into stronger beings.

Within you there are some elements that will determine the degree of success of the visualization, in a given situation:

Desire, faith, acceptance; be aware that the river of life sometimes takes a tortuous course before taking you to your goal.

The natural state of life is one of flux and constant change. By understanding this, we tune into its rhythm and become able to give and take freely, as we never really lose anything and are constantly winning.

When you become aware of this mental field that exists, you will notice creativity flowing in a more outcropped way, that's the secret.

Roadmap to boost creativity

The following techniques were developed by Dr. Flash, Dr. Morris (2009) and other psychologists and psychiatrists to help people break free from routine constraints and use innate creativity to develop new projects, find problem solutions, and adapt to change.

You can use these steps in your own life for whatever you want to create:

Get ready: read and talk as much as you can about what you want to create — a solution, a framework, a new approach to a business. Prepare the ground.
Incube: We all want quick fixes, but when the answers don't come right away, put the idea to rest.

Let it brew in the subconscious.

Later, maybe a week or a month later, there will be progress.

Light yourself up: in cartoons this is represented by a light bulb over the head. This is the point at which progress occurs. Let it happen. Something pops into your head, and you say, "Oh, that's a good idea."

Test: once the creative solution is found, it is necessary to apply it. If there's a new way of dealing with your marriage, for example, put it into practice. If there's a new way to create a sculpture, do it. The Doctor. Flach (2009) says that no one receives the Nobel Prize for having a new idea, but for testing it and
prove it works.

Distance yourself: You can accomplish this just by changing the room you work in or your clothes. You can go on a "mind tour," imagining a pleasant trip or a place you would like to go. Contemplate images far removed from your common interests or work.

Vary leisure activities: Don't devote your free time to a single hobby, such as tennis or watching television. Acquire a diversity of experiences. Meet new people. Read books. First of all, leisure

should relax you. It's hard to be creative when tense. And, avoiding

the tennis or TV only routine, you get

stimuli from various people and environments, in addition to using a

range of muscles and talents.

Variety is a fertilizer for creativity. Find

security. it's very difficult to be creative if you're worried about

survival.

Anxiety blocks the free flow of creativity.

Choose the companies: carefully. Walking in the company of people

who are constantly putting you down, criticizing you, you will not be

able to create.

Don't be afraid to be alone: if you're going to be creative, you need

time to listen to yourself rather than someone or something else.

Try to slow down the engine: it takes some quiet, idle time to let the

thought process work. This implies daydreaming, a form of mental

activity not looked upon favorably by parents and teachers —

however, useful and capable of opening new channels. You can also remember and allow

Past successes and failures float through the mind for reassessment.

Keep a pencil and notebook handy: to capture fleeting ideas that may later prove valuable.

You never know what connections will be established between what is new to you and what you commonly do.

Discover your best time: the biological rhythm influences you. At a time of day or night when you are at your best. You probably know what it is, but if you want to be sure, it's possibly the time when your body temperature is at its highest.

Discover your best place: try to remember where you had your best ideas.

Some like to think in a warm bath and others while walking or working with their hands.

Write or record your frustrations: when you are frustrated or confused, and ideas don'tappear, write or record what upsets you. This will help "put the house in order for action".

Cultivate your brain: Verbalize or write down as many ideas as you can extract from your brain. Let your mind wander and think of all kinds of solutions. You can help yourself hit fertile ground by establishing analogies. For example, "I want to paint a better picture, but it's like squeezing the last bit of paste out of the tube."

The dawn of creativity: in this technique, you put the main goal in the center of the others or in the "sun".

Try a new approach. If you don't fail, you're not being creative, as the new trails have no signposts and are full of traps.

Lastly, don't make excuses: age, illness and lack of time are frequently offered reasons for the inability to create. Rarely are they substantiated.

Picasso, aged 91, kept art paraphernalia by his bed in case he woke up during the night and had a good idea.

the google case

Google was founded by Larry Page and Sergey Brin, two Stanford PhD students in 1998.

The private company announced in June 1999 that it had secured $25 million in equity consolidation.

Its partners include Kleiner Perkins Caufield & Byers and Sequoia Capital. Google provides services through its public website, www.google.com. Google's mission is to provide the best Internet search options by making the world's information accessible and useful. Google, developer of the world's largest search engine, offers the fastest and easiest way to find information on the web and in administration.

However, anyone who thinks that life there is easy is wrong. This informal environment serves to encourage the creativity of a team that works hard to achieve results. There is strong pressure to increase the audience of search engines and videos on the internet, in addition to charging for prospecting new customers.

In Brazil, Google has around 200 employees at its headquarters in São Paulo - working especially in the commercial and administrative areas - and another 60 in Belo Horizonte, where the team of engineers, programmers and product managers, responsible for creating tools and new products. "The physical environment is the least important, because other companies also offer attractions.

The difference here is the culture, the freedom to determine where and how you want to work", says Felix Ximenes, responsible for the group's communication.

Bosses delegate tasks and goals, but the way to achieve them is up to each one, as long as the expected performance is achieved. If the employee plays a game of pool at three in the afternoon and goes back to highly productive work, that's what matters in the company's philosophy.

Frank dialogue, constant work in multifunctional and multicultural teams, opportunities for rapid growth and building an international career are other factors that weigh in favor of the company. The turnover rate is low: less than 1% leaves for the competition. "Google speaks the same language as young people. They don't want to have barriers between the professional and the personal", says the president of the Cia. de Talentos, Sofia Esteves, responsible for the research.

Strengths -

Ángel Jiménez de Luis, editor of the blog Gadgetoblog of Diario El Mundo (2010), paid a visit to the Google company in Zurich (Switzerland) and showed how the employees work there. The quality of work and life found in the internet giant is fantastic.

Check out:

• It has a slide that connects the offices on the first floor to the cafeteria and gym. No need to wait for the elevator, just slip on.

• Employees' children are welcome. There is a special place for children.

• All employees eat very well during working hours and because of that there is a sports gym on the ground floor for them to burn extra calories.

• On each floor there are at least two rest areas with food and drinks, also free.

• Each employee manages his own time and work. There are no fixed schedules, only delivery deadlines, which obviously must be met. You can stop at any time to play video games or pool, etc.

• In this workplace. Employees are free to change tables at any time if they feel like it, exchange ideas, designs, suggestions.

• Google also has the water lounge, a place of peace used for relaxation. There are massage chairs and dim lighting. Employees go there to sleep or rest before a stressful meeting. With wonderful armchairs.

• The meeting rooms are named after famous television series and movies. These igloos are located in the Star Wars area. They are authentic refuges that were used in scientific missions in Antarctica.

• The company also has a large library which many claim to be the most beautiful and surprising part of the building. There, in addition to many books and a huge kitchen, employees can relax in front of a virtual fireplace. A current Google employee says it's a great place to work. These are the things I like about my job:

• Everyone is super smart. There are 18 different types of coffee.

• Free snack, lunch and dinner. Food is gourmet quality (eg omelette shop, chefs who make custom sandwiches for you, sashimi, free drinks and snacks 24/7).

• Every Friday, Larry, Sergei, or Eric (the highest in the company hierarchy) comes up to us personally and asks what our doubts and questions are. "On that day we also have free beer"

Marcos Coronato in an interview with Luiz Barroso (interview by telephone), one of the eight Google employees in the world to hold the title of "distinguished engineer", a 46-year-old from Rio de Janeiro, lives in the United States.

This means that, among the 10,000 people who work for the largest internet company in the world, Barroso is a highly renowned or outstanding engineer. It is the highest position that someone can reach in the company, equivalent to a vice president, only in the technological career.

In reality, what impresses is the speed with which things go on Google. The company's mentality is that everyone attacks the problems, tries to solve them, tries to be more useful. Access to information on Google is essential. There is transparency in the company. An engineer in the United States would have a hard time hiding information from a colleague in Europe.

You need to show what you're doing, how you're moving forward. We do this in "weekly sniplets", a weekly summary of the work. It's very practical, five or six topics, it can be the amount of information that fits on a Powerpoint slide. This is documentation that is available to the entire company. No other company can share so much information with so many employees. There is an exchange there: everyone benefits, but there is a risk of someone exposing that information. Google works with ongoing employee education to preserve this culture.

Negative points -

Fernando Martines (2010) interviewed some Google employees (who preferred to remain anonymous), and discovered some more news:

Claims a former Google employee (prefers to remain anonymous) says, "I was there for about five years. You can read about the good parts anywhere, so I'll try to offer a counterpoint based on having worked on other software companies" (former Google employee).

• A common problem is that it's not easy to lose focus and get bogged down by all the perks. It's embarrassing to be around people who have become like spoiled brats.

• Google headquarters in Mountain View, California. there's a specific engineering problem, is that there's a lot of support there for operations — that is, a lot of people whose job it is to keep the systems running. And engineers are often not available any time you want to call them. The upside is that they can focus on development, get adequate sleep, and be more productive.

• The downside is that they can easily lose touch with what is really happening in the data centers and sometimes even with their customers.

Finally, the company is betting big on "production luck," which means trying a bunch of things in a variety of areas in the hope that some of those attempts will pay off.

• Management work within the company is terrible. A typical manager has 50 to 100 employees, so even if they meet with their subordinates once a month for 30 minutes, that's not a lot of time for interaction. As a result, managers are not empowered to participate in technical decisions, they don't have much say in performance reviews (this is done by another committee), and they don't even influence hiring (which is also done by a committee).

Senior Google employees were asked what managers actually do, and everyone's answer was, "I don't know." Almost every managerial decision I witnessed at Google (mostly around resource mobilization for new projects) was not good.

The only way I could explain their position is some sort of politics and infighting at the top. "If you like being a technical manager, if that's how you see your career, Google is definitely not for you."

Sergio Montini (2010), a former Google employee, states: "(I work at a search engine competing with Google, Ask.com) here in London, but we have a partnership with Google".

After lunch, which usually has repeats, I'm always invited to a game of foosball.(pimbolin), and next thing I know I've already killed my afternoon. "I have nothing left but to eat even more there, and all for free."

Three co-workers left Google to work for us, I wonder why on earth anyone would leave all the perks to a smaller company? The answer is unanimous, over time you lose focus and realize that it's Google's way of locking you into it.

Creativity Methods

A creativity process requires efforts, whether by an individual or a team, and can result in new projects, products and ideas, which can be applied in practice.

Creative thinking is usually associated with divergent thinking, as it involves unusual ideas and experiments that coin several original possibilities (KING; SCHLICKSUPP, 1999).

Creative capacity can be stimulated through the environment, techniques and tools. An environment created to welcome creative ideas without criticism, it offers a climate of freedom that encourages the development of ideas and the conception of new perspectives and ways of interpreting reality.

Teamwork is a measure that favors the performance of mental processes, due to the exchange of heterogeneous and unique information and knowledge for each individual (KING;

SCHLICKSUPP, 1999). In the process of generating ideas, the sum of the skills and experiences of each employee tends to aggregate and enhance collective performance. However, for a better use of the individual creative performance of the members, it is important to mediate the creativity process through a method that connects these members synergistically, taking advantage of the creative potential of the group, to the maximum. King and Schlicksupp (1999) emphasize that teamwork, with good performance, commonly becomes self-sustaining due to the quality achieved in the results.

Mainemelis and Ronson (2006) analyzed organizational behavior as a game, in a study that promoted the relationship between play and creativity. For the authors, the act of playing stimulates the development of creativity in the organizational field, although many organizations still consider the game only as a matter of distraction.

The game can foster the ability to recombine existing elements and promote integration among participants, which is a desirable situation to encourage the act of creativity, as discussed by King and Schlicksupp (1999). A game as engagement stimulates creativity through the cognitive and affective dimensions that involve it. Studies carried out in the field of cognitive psychology have shown that the game involves a large amount of mental transformations and divergent thinking, as it stimulates the imaginary and the symbolic (MAINEMELIS; RONSON, 2006).

The game, in the work environment, allows individuals to develop their skills, exploring their skills through challenges.

From another point of view, the integration that occurs through a game in the work environment, in addition to promoting creativity, can represent a strategy for employees to spontaneously contribute ideas that, in another situation, they would not feel safe to expose.

Gurteen (1998) also makes the association between creativity and a game, reporting that a creativity process plays with words, concepts and also metaphors, without borders or limitations.

The essence of this game, for Gurteen (1998), is that nothing is static or unalterable.

Every interaction in our lives can be seen as a game, and the business world is no different.

The game begins with social interactions, based on the understanding that the exchange of experiences and knowledge are learning opportunities that stimulate our cognitive abilities.

This process encourages creativity by relating known elements to new elements. Corroborating the above, King and Schlicksupp (1999) state that the use of processes or techniques for problem solving in an organization is highly effective in stimulating creative thinking and learning. Organizations can choose between several existing models, and often the processes that represent the organizational structure come with predetermined phases, like in a game. Aiming to contribute to the conception of the creativity process, these authors suggest the application of techniques that support the problem definition phase and later the generation of ideas.

In this sense, creativity techniques can contribute, in a relevant way, to the creative solution of problems, as they provide the effervescence of ideas through insights and the flexibility of thought, by challenging conventional assumptions, supporting interdisciplinarity and also by allowing reorganizing processes. elements of a problem.

Creativity techniques can favor the innovation process, contributing to the creative process to define the problem and also to select and develop ideas in practice.

compass technique

A relatively simple and effective technique is the Compass, used to support the definition of problems and its main utility is to provide a broad exposure of the previously chosen problem (CLEGG; BIRCH, 2000).

The technique consists of, initially, making a statement about the problem to be investigated based on: "why?".

The answers obtained are noted down, and the same question is used again for each one of them, obtaining, in this way, new answers, applying the same question, until the alternative answers to the question proposed are exhausted.
It is understood that, in this way, it will be possible to arrive at a new configuration of the problem that has more relevance than its initial description.

This technique allows thinking about the problem from different perspectives, as new elements emerge with each question-answer cycle.

Davidson and Sternberg (2003) complement the above, stating that the thought that diverges and questions what is taken as truth, allows a critical process that contributes to the definition of the problem in a more concise way, as it aims to exhaust the doubts that may arise when question why.

These elements may be inhibited by the initial statement and are approached over time with this line of thought.

Brainstorm

Brainstorming was created in 1939 by Alex Osborn and means, in his conception, brain to create ideas to solve a problem (OSBORN, 1954).

This technique, which assists in the process of generating ideas, emerged from the analysis of the causes that prevented the effectiveness of a meeting, and made it possible to determine a set of behaviors aimed at reducing distractions and enhancing the creative result for problem solutions.

The main objective of Brainstorming is to find solutions to problems, based on the knowledge that the group has. Its main premise is the assumption that all ideas have the same value. More than a creativity technique, it can be considered as a way of creating a new cultural paradigm, as it ensures that individuals do not work in isolation and seek solutions in collective wisdom.

The technique is normally applied when the problem requires a new concept or alternative solutions within a knowledge area.

Brainstorming can be applied even when available time is limited. It does not require prior knowledge of the technique, not even in-depth knowledge of the problem.

On the other hand, due to these characteristics, it requires a larger group of members, so that it is possible to generate a greater variety of ideas.

The technique is described by King and Schlicksupp (1999) in 4 main steps:

1- identify the appropriate group to manage the Brainstorming, based on the knowledge and experience of each individual.

2- present the rules and establish the topics and objectives.

3- Brainstorming, generating as many ideas as possible.

4- transcribe and make the ideas clear and, later, conclude by selecting those that best suit the objective.

Brainstorming has as a rule not to judge ideas as good or bad during the process, as the initial purpose is quantity and not quality. It is understood that any type of previous judgment could inhibit the creative capacity of the members by mental block in defense of the criticism, for supposedly bad ideas. Ideas provided by members in a Brainstorming session do not allow copyright, they must be provided with the intention of being modified and developed by the group.

This technique aims to release creativity and share ideas, apparently unusual, with the group, without worrying whether the idea will be good or bad, used or not. In this circumstance, spontaneity is valued.

The Brainstorming session must be conducted by a facilitator, who can make comments or questions that facilitate creative thinking in moments of silence, which are called dead point, that is, when the

group's stock of ideas runs out. The session can have several

phases until the thinking is deepened and more specific ideas are

developed.

challenging assumptions

Challenging assumptions is a technique that starts from the premise that being creative is breaking with assumptions, consolidated and accepted without rational justification. It aims to assist in solving problems with the generation of ideas. This technique does not require a large team, and can be used individually and for as long as necessary.

The application of the technique consists of exposing the problem or need, identifying the main hypothesis as a solution, a priori.

Clegg and Birch report that it is not always possible to identify assumptions clearly, but challenging them when identified makes it easier to reveal the real problem. The authors suggest working with one assumption at a time, to make what was previously confusing clearer and more specific and only change assumptions when the previous analysis alternatives are exhausted.

Challenging established assumptions breaks thought patterns, makes the employee seek innovative solutions.

Divergent thinking contributes to the diversity of ideas, and is valued for its ability to contribute to the conception of original ideas.

opposite technique

Opposite is a creativity technique that aims to identify the opposite aspects of what is intended to be done. As an example, if you want to improve a process in the company, identify which aspects would aggravate that process. As Clegg and Birch explain, it is possible that these negative aspects are being practiced in the organization. Identifying the nuances of opposing thinking offers a unique possibility to explore the frontier of thought, because when you reach the point of exhaustion of ideas to solve a problem, trying the opposite can be positive, by changing your point of view about it.

It is worth noting that this technique does not require a large team to perform it, nor prior knowledge of the technique. To start, a Brainstorming session should be carried out to identify the negative aspects that could aggravate the problem.

After identifying these aspects, they must be analyzed and studied how to modify or prevent these actions from occurring.

It is suggested to divide the group into two teams. One of the teams must report the positive aspects of an idea and the members of the second team must oppose the idea, highlighting the negative aspects. By exploring the positive and negative aspects from the contributions of the participants, from both groups, it tends to obtain a significant amount of ideas that can offer relevant elements for the conception of the solution to the problem.

The human being is not the traveller, he is the path.

Creativity manifests itself in different ways and in different fields of knowledge.

It is not something new, nor is it exclusive to the field of arts, communication or design. Creative behavior is something inherent to human beings, observable from the simplest tasks, such as improvising or changing something in everyday life, to more complex tasks, such as conceiving new theories in the field of science.

The restriction that human beings themselves create is what often limits the possibility of better use of information for the development of creative capacity.
Creativity techniques contribute to eliminating such barriers and favoring the fervor of creative acts. The techniques are diverse and thought from different points of view, in general, all are appropriate

to apply in organizations, subject only to the unique characteristics of the team that will use them and the purpose of use.

In general, it is understood that in order to achieve good results, when it comes to creativity, the synergy between team members is effectively positive, this becomes noticeable in the comparison between creative and traditional sectors, as in the case of the communication sector, which has more development and prestige work dynamics than others, facilitating this synergy when ideas are conceived.

Thinking about a problem in isolation, using a creativity technique can bring good results, but thinking collectively is actually more effective, as each individual will think in a unique way and will complement the vision of the whole.

It should be noted, however, that if creativity techniques alone do not generate results, the human factor is essential for their operation. Yet "the human" is not a constant in a formula, but a non-mathematical variable, a fundamental cultural variable.

The listed techniques do not address motivational factors or even creative thinking skills and the individual's specialty, perhaps for this reason it is stated that creativity is impaired in organizations, as the techniques are suggested for their application without highlighting the need to consider the singularities of the collaborators who will carry out the creativity processes.

In this sense, I highlight the importance of individuals who carry out the creativity processes.

When analyzing these proposed techniques, would these methods be aseptic?

What if the focus is on the people rather than the process?

It is the incredible social and rational ability of human beings that makes the creative process possible and not just a set of blindly applied techniques.

Finally, understand one thing!

Things are constantly changing and the creative culture must be prepared to adapt to these changes.

"There is something else that bears repeating: for creativity to emerge, we must loosen controls, take risks, trust our colleagues, work to pave the way, and pay attention to anything that scares them. All these things will not make managing a creative culture any easier. but the ease
it is not the goal; but rather excellence".

Apply the learning that was given in this material and you will realize great benefits.

From now on…

You are no longer the same, since you started reading this material, you have become a different person…

Enjoy!

Who is Matheus Martins Soares?

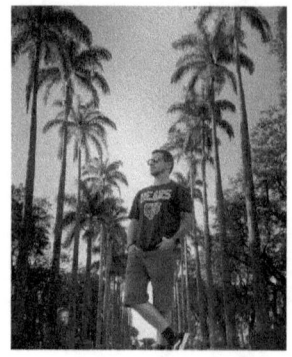

Matheus is an Ex-Military / Presidential Agent, graduated in Marketing since 2018 and specialist in copywriting. He has written for more than 27 different niches, showing his ability to adapt to different topics and audiences.

Throughout his career, he has worked in large companies, such as the largest business magazine in the country and the largest marketing consultancy in Brazil. Contributed to the success of important campaigns, generating + 30mm in sales for its customers. Published over 100 books on Amazon and gained readers in over 10 different countries. An expert in StoryTelling and UX Writing, he also works behind the scenes as a GhostWriter, giving voice to other people's ideas and stories. His method is capable of writing a book in less than 24 hours.

With a strategic vision and knowledge in marketing, he helps

companies, authors and literary projects to achieve success.

He found himself in the world of marketing, writing and human

behavior, his ability to adapt to different challenges is a

differential that makes him stand out in his field.